Martin Luther King Jr.

by Jonatha A. Brown

Reading consultant: Susan Nations, M.Ed., author/literacy coach/consultant

WR WEEKLY READER

EARLY LEARNING LIBRARY

Please visit our web site at: www.earlyliteracy.cc
For a free color catalog describing Weekly Reader® Early Learning Library's list
of high-quality books, call 1-877-445-5824 (USA) or 1-800-387-3178 (Canada).
Weekly Reader® Early Learning Library's fax: (414) 336-0164.

Library of Congress Cataloging-in-Publication Data

Brown, Jonatha A.
    Martin Luther King Jr. / by Jonatha A. Brown.
      p. cm. — (People we should know)
    Includes bibliographical references and index.
    ISBN 0-8368-4467-X (lib. bdg.)
    ISBN 0-8368-4474-2 (softcover)
    1. King, Martin Luther, Jr., 1929-1968—Juvenile literature. 2. African Americans—Biography—Juvenile
literature. 3. Civil rights workers—United States—Biography—Juvenile literature. 4. Baptists—United
States—Clergy—Biography—Juvenile literature. 4. African Americans—Civil rights—History—20th century—
Juvenile literature. I. Title. II. People we should know (Milwaukee, Wis.)
E185.97.K5B75   2005
323'.092—dc22
    [B]   2004057239

This edition first published in 2005 by
Weekly Reader® Early Learning Library
330 West Olive Street, Suite 100
Milwaukee, WI 53212 USA

Copyright © 2005 by Weekly Reader® Early Learning Library

Based on *Martin Luther King Jr.* (Trailblazers of the Modern World series) by Adele Q. Brown
Editor: JoAnn Early Macken
Designer: Scott M. Krall
Picture researcher: Diane Laska-Swanke

Photo credits: Cover, title, pp. 4, 10, 13, 17, 20, 21 © AP/Wide World Photos; p. 7
© William Lovelace/Express/Getty Images; pp. 5, 9 © Hulton Archive/Getty Images; p. 15
© Shel Hershorn/Hulton Archive/Getty Images; p. 16 © Walker Evans/Library of Congress/
Getty Images; p. 19 © MPI/Hulton Archive/Getty Images

Printed in the United States of America

1 2 3 4 5 6 7 8 9 09 08 07 06 05

Table of Contents

Words that appear in the glossary are printed in **boldface**
type the first time they occur in the text.

Chapter 1: Childhood

Martin Luther King Jr. was born on January 15, 1929. When he was born, his name was Michael, just like his father's. When he was four years old, his father changed both of their names to Martin. Then the boy became Martin Luther King Jr. He was called M. L. for short.

Martin Luther King Jr. was born in this house.

Martin's family was black. Mrs. King was a teacher. Dr. King was the **pastor** of a church. They had three children. Their daughter Chris was the oldest. Then came Martin and then his brother Alfred Daniel. They lived in Atlanta, Georgia.

In the South, black people and white people did not mix. They lived in different parts of town. They went to different schools. Most public places were **segregated**. One area was for white people. Another was for black people. The white area was always nicer.

Segregation was unfair. It

Most black people in Atlanta lived in run-down old houses.

made black people feel bad. But they did not dare complain. They were afraid white people would punish them. So they lived in poorer neighborhoods. They went to poorer schools. They kept their mouths shut.

A Brief Friendship

Young Martin once had a white friend. The friendship did not last long. The other boy's parents did not want their son to play with a black child. The boys could not be friends anymore. Martin felt very hurt. This was his first experience with **racism**.

Martin's mother told him about slavery and racism. "You are as good as anyone else," she said. "Don't ever forget that."

All three King children sang in the church choir. They all played piano, too. Their mother taught them to read. Religion was always a big part of their family life.

Martin was a smart boy who loved to read. School was easy for him. He skipped two grades. He graduated from high school when he was only fifteen.

This man would not let a black woman into a white waiting room.

Chapter 2: College and Family

Martin started college in 1944. He went to Morehouse College in Atlanta. The students there were black. The teachers were black, too.

North and South

During the summers, Martin worked. His first summer job was in Connecticut. He worked in the tobacco fields. It was his first trip to the North. He found that black people mixed more freely with white people there. They went to the same schools. They ate in the same restaurants. They shopped at the same stores. Martin was surprised to see that, but he liked it.

When summer ended, Martin went back to Atlanta. It was hard for him to go back to the old ways. He did not like being treated badly just

In the South, many poor black children had to help their parents work in the fields.

because he was black. But he did not know what to do about it. The next summer, he worked in Atlanta. He saw that black people there were paid less than white people for the same work. He started thinking about how he could work for change.

Martin graduated from college in 1948. He was nineteen years old. That year, he became a minister. His father wanted Martin to help him at church.

Martin and Coretta Scott King are shown here in 1956.

But Martin wanted to continue his schooling. He studied religion in Pennsylvania for three years. Then he went to Boston University. He read books written by great people. He thought about their ideas and wrote about them. He thought about using **nonviolent** ways to change things. He also began to give sermons at local churches. He was known as a good speaker.

While he was in Boston, Martin met Coretta Scott. They fell in love. They married on June 18, 1953. Martin soon finished his studies. When he graduated, he became Dr. Martin Luther King Jr.

In 1954, Martin took a job in Montgomery, Alabama. He was pastor of the Dexter Avenue Baptist Church. He and Coretta started a family.

Martin's Children

Martin and Coretta had four children. Yolanda was born first. Then the Kings had a baby boy. They named him Martin Luther III. A few years later, Dexter and Bernice were born.

Chapter 3: Bus Boycott

In December 1955, Martin's world changed. The change began on a city bus in Montgomery. A black woman named Rosa Parks rode the bus that day. A white man got on the bus after her. The bus driver told Rosa Parks to give her seat to the white man. The driver told her to sit in the back of the bus. Mrs. Parks refused. The driver called the police. They arrested Mrs. Parks.

A Plan for Change

This arrest was big news in the black part of the city. Black leaders met to talk about it. Martin was one of them. They were tired of being treated unfairly. They wanted to be treated with respect. They tried to think of ways to solve the problem.

Martin and the others came up with a plan. The black people in the city would stop riding city buses. They would **boycott** the bus company. The bus company would lose money. Then it might agree to treat black people fairly. The leaders knew the plan might not work. Still, it was worth a try.

On December 5, 1955, the boycott began. The city buses were nearly empty. That night, Martin

Martin was a great speaker. He told black people they would win in the end. He asked them not to give up hope.

spoke to a big crowd. He asked the people to keep the boycott going. He said it would not be easy. He warned that white people might get angry. Some whites might yell at black people or try to hurt them. But he said they must stay calm. They must not fight back. Fighting would just cause more problems.

Time and Effort

The crowd listened to Martin. They respected his words. They agreed to keep up the boycott. Day after day, black people did not ride the buses. Some black people walked to work or to school. Some rode bicycles. Others got rides from friends with cars. They stayed off the buses.

The local white people noticed. Some got angry. They did not want black people to stand up for themselves. They did not want to share the best seats on the bus, either. Some tried to scare the black people into ending the boycott. They yelled. They threw things. Someone even threw a bomb into Martin's home! The Kings were not hurt, and Martin told people not to fight back.

The boycott lasted more than a year. It made the news all over the country. Finally, the U.S. Supreme Court stepped in. The court said that segregation on buses was against the law. Martin and his friends had won! Black people no longer had to give up their bus seats to white people.

Young black people tried to order food at a white lunch counter.

Chapter 4: A Great Leader

In 1957, Martin spoke to thousands of people in Washington, D.C.

By 1957, Martin was famous. His name was on the news. His picture was in the newspapers. His voice was on TV and radio. He made many speeches. He said that skin color does not make some people better than others. He said racism is wrong. Segregation is wrong. He said the world would be a better place without those things. He asked people to work for change.

Black people heard Martin's words. White people heard them, too. Most people agreed it was time for change. Many **civil rights** groups joined together. They formed the Southern Christian Leadership Council (SCLC). The new group asked Martin to lead it. He became the president of the SCLC.

Martin worked very hard. He wrote books about equal rights. He spoke in public. He traveled all over the United States. But he did not have time to do all those things and be a church pastor, too. In 1959, he made a choice. He left his job as pastor.

He and his family moved to Atlanta, Georgia. Martin was back in the city of his birth. On some Sundays, he preached at his father's church. Most of the time, he worked for the SCLC.

Working for Equal Rights

In 1963, Martin visited Birmingham, Alabama. He led a big **protest** against segregation. Thousands of people joined him. They boycotted stores that did not treat blacks fairly. They marched through the city. They carried signs that called for equal rights.

Some of the city's leaders were racists. They did not like the protest. They put Martin and other black leaders in jail. They put children in jail, too. They used fire hoses to break up the marches. They turned police dogs on the crowds.

Many people were scared. Some were hurt. They kept up the protests, anyway. They did not fight back. Finally, the store owners of Birmingham gave in. They agreed to treat blacks and whites equally. It was a great success for Martin and his friends.

White people began to join blacks in their marches for equal rights.

Martin received the Nobel Peace Prize for his work.

In 1964, Martin was awarded the Nobel Peace Prize. That was a great honor. By then, the push for equal rights was very strong. The U.S. Congress even passed a law that gave equal voting rights to blacks. Martin was pleased.

Martin's life was very full. But it was not very long. He died on April 4, 1968. On that day, he was shot and killed by a racist.

Many people cried. They were very sad. But they

Martin Luther King Jr. Day

The third Monday in January is Martin Luther King Jr. Day. It is a national holiday. On that day, we honor Martin. We talk about his ideas. We talk about how he helped people.

did not stop working for civil rights. Some people worked even harder. Their work paid off. They helped make laws that protect our rights, no matter what our skin color. They kept Martin's memory alive.

Glossary

boycott — to refuse to use a service or buy a product

civil rights — rights of all people to vote and to live and work where they choose

nonviolent — not using force or causing damage or injury

pastor — leader of a church

protest — to speak out against something

racism — treating people differently because of the color of their skin

segregated — separated, kept apart

For More Information

Books

Martin Luther King Jr.: A Man Who Changed Things. Rookie Biographies (series). Carol Greene (Scholastic Library)

Martin Luther King Jr. and the March on Washington. Frances E. Ruffin (Grosset & Dunlap)

Martin Luther King, Jr. Day: Honoring a Man of Peace. Finding Out About Holidays (series). Carol Gnojewski (Enslow)

My Dream of Martin Luther King. Faith Ringgold (Knopf)

Web Sites

Kulture Kidz: Black History from A-Z
www.aakulturezone.com/kidz/abc/mlk.html
Notes about Martin's life and part of his most famous speech

Martin Luther King, Jr. Day On the Net
www.holidays.net/mlk/
Read about Martin, Rosa Parks, and more

Index

About the Author

Jonatha A. Brown has written several books for children. She lives in Phoenix, Arizona, with her husband and two dogs. If you happen to come by when she isn't at home working on a book, she's probably out riding or visiting with one of her horses. She may be gone for quite a while, so you'd better come back later.